MINISTRY OF THE TOWEL

"Serving God By Serving Others."

T. Cedric Brown

MAC Publishing

Published by:
MAC Publishing
www.macpub.org

MINISTRY OF THE TOWEL
ISBN-10: 0989248054
ISBN-13: 978-0-9892480-5-1

TABLE OF CONTENTS

ACKNOWLEDGMENTS

ac·knowl·edg·ment [ik-na-lij-ment] noun - an expression of appreciation.

First and foremost, I want to express my appreciation to my Lord and Savior Jesus Christ for His strength and grace to complete this project. I want to extend my sincerest gratitude to my lovely wife, Lady Bobette Brown, for your prayers, encouragement, wisdom, and for being a constant source of inspiration. You are the wind beneath my wings. To my sons, Joshua and Caleb: thank you for your love and support. I am so proud to be your father. To the best mother a son could have, Eleanor Brown, thank you for the many life lessons you taught me. I would not be who I am had it not been for you.

To my spiritual father, Bishop Alfred A. Owens, Jr., thank you for being a true example of leadership. Your mentorship and friendship has had a profound impact on my life. I am forever indebted to you. To Co-Pastor Susie Owens, your teaching and preaching has inspired and challenged me to become a better minister of the Gospel. Thank you for sowing into my life. To my church family, Greater Mt. Calvary Holy Church, thank you for your encouragement, love, and your "amens."

FOREWORD

Bishop Terrence Cedric Brown is a man of God, after God's own heart. I thank God continuously for joining him to my life, the ministry of Greater Mt. Calvary Holy Church and to the Legacy of the Mt. Calvary Holy Church of America, Inc. and to the Body of Christ.

I have watched him grow, develop and mature to a servant, humble in spirit, rich in faith, and faithful in service. Bishop Brown began his ministry as deacon, a minister, and a Sunday school teacher, Elder, Bible Study teacher, Armor Bearer, Adjutant, Associate Pastor, Bishop and Vice Bishop, all the while choosing to serve others than to be served.

Because he has the true spirit of a servant, this book could be penned by none greater than himself, whose example of being used as a "towel" has been demonstrated down through the 25+ years he has ***served*** in ministry. Bishop Brown can write so meaningfully on the ministry of the towel because he is an example of the same.

Bishop Brown is most beneficial in God's hands because like a towel, he is ***bendable.*** He is not one to dictate how he will be used. I have witnessed his flexibilities combined with his adaptability which highlights his ***bendability***. He is able to serve and be faithful regardless of the protocol in which he is assigned. Not only is Brown ***bendable,*** but he is most ***dependable***. I have been able to count on him in many and varied situations. He is solid like a rock; he means what he says and does what he says. He has never tried to usurp his authority, and even in occasions where he disagreed, he, nonetheless, carried out the task as best he could. Like a towel, whatever Brown is called to do, he is ***dependable*** to see it through.

A towel is also ***sendable***. It is sent without question. Wherever the hand takes it, it goes. Brown has not been anxious about God's timing. Many went, but only a few were sent. He has always been conscious of God's lead and has felt contentment in his leader sending him out. God has opened numerous doors for his ministry gifts, but he has accepted none without my approval and blessing! Whether the mountain high, or the valley low. Brown has been ***sendable*** at all times.

A towel does not take offense if it gets dirty or torn while being used. I have observed Bishop Brown under pressure, stress, and distress. But because he is able to recover quietly from iniquity, he knows the value of being ***mendable***. Faced with major ministry and personal challenges, he has remained focused and has not allowed anger or bitterness to consume him. He remains the same! I have watched him take a licking and keep on ticking! He is most ***mendable***.

Without reservation or hesitation, Bishop Brown is like a towel: ***bendable, dependable, sendable***, and ***mendable.*** These qualities made him ***expendable***. His testimony "Give myself away" to be used to the glory of God as a servant has caused him to be a tremendous blessing to the Kingdom.

I am most proud to endorse and promote my Joshua (Moses), my Jonathan (David), my Timothy (Paul), my son. You will be blessed by this book!

Because of Calvary,

Bishop Alfred A. Owens, Jr.

INTRODUCTION

May I Help You?

Walk into any restaurant, department store or "mom & pop" shop and the first question they ask is, "May I help you" or "How can I help you?" or "What can I get you today?" or even "How may I serve you?" Service, we all want it. Everyone desires to be served. We buy products and services based upon the level of customer service the company provides. The sale of products from companies has declined not because of the product itself, but because of the lack of customer service provided by the company. Corporations spend millions of dollars training their employees in the area of customer relations. Because they realize that obtaining, retaining, and maintaining customers is the key to sustaining profitability in the competitive world of business. As it is in the secular, so it is in the sacred. Ministry is about providing customer service, not for profit in terms of dollars and cents, but to glorify God. Jesus Christ teaches us, through precept and example, the art of serving.

The Greatest Server Of All Time

Everybody's looking for a hero, everybody's looking for someone to emulate, to copy. We are looking for someone to pattern ourselves after. There is nothing wrong with that. One preacher said that there is nothing wrong with being a copycat as long as you copy the right cat. There's nothing wrong with looking at individuals and desiring to be like them. We observe traits, characteristics in them that we want in us. There is nothing wrong with aspiring to be a better a person, a person of character. The greatest example given to mankind is Jesus Christ. If you want to know how to conduct yourself, if you want a pattern for living your life, if you are looking for a model to follow in effectively handling life's situations, Jesus Christ is your greatest example. Even in serving, Jesus is our greatest model. Jesus states in Matthew 20:28:

"Even as the Son of man came not to be ministered unto, but to minister, and to give his life a ransom for many."

We are called to serve God. That is our mission, our calling, our purpose. Serving God is expressed when we serve others. Whether we teach, feed the homeless, clothe the naked, or usher; whether we are a musician, secretary, administrator, clergy, counselor, pastor, or bishop, God has called us to serve Him through helping others. Our gifts, talents and abilities are not just for personal gain. But we are gifted to help someone, to teach someone, to encourage someone. In return, we are blessed, nourished, encouraged, inspired and fulfilled; filled to the full, satisfied, and content. We are living in a time when becoming filled to the full is based upon selfish gain. The irony is that we are not full; we are not satisfied. We are still empty. We strive for things and pleasures and still come up empty. The Bible says if you try to save your life, you will lose it, but if you lose your life for Christ's sake you will find it (Matt. 16:25). A purpose-filled life is a life that gives willingly and sacrificially to others for the betterment of others.

In the 13th chapter of John, Jesus is having supper with his disciples. This is their last time of fellowship before He is crucified. Jesus could have said so many things during this last supper. Knowing that this was the last time they would be together, what would be His parting words? What life principle did He want to leave with them? Since this was the last supper, we can suppose that whatever He said, whatever principle He wanted to drive home, it was significant, it was important, it was life-changing. Would Jesus talk about faith? Would He talk about prosperity or how to preach? No! The lesson He teaches is serving. Out of all the things Jesus could have taught, He teaches, by precept and example, a lesson on serving one another. Let's look at Jesus' lesson on serving.

The Bible states that Jesus rises from supper, takes off His robe, puts on a towel, pours water in a basin, and He washes the feet of all the disciples.

In the Greek language, the word towel means "apron." In other words, Jesus puts on an apron and began to wash feet. Imagine Jesus removing His robe, putting on a towel or an apron and washing dirty feet. The apron is worn by servants. It is part of the attire of a servant. God has called each of us to serve. In God's Kingdom, there are two callings.

He initially calls us to salvation. He summons us to accept Christ as Lord and Savior. Accepting Jesus into our hearts is not the end. We don't sit and "take our rest." He then calls us to service. He calls us to go to work in the kingdom. God always calls you *from* something *to* something. He calls us from darkness to light, he called Abraham from Haran to "a land I will show you." Once we answer the call of salvation, then we must answer the call of service.

Ministry is more than preaching. The word minister is defined as to wait on tables; to run errands; to perform menial tasks; to be attentive, in other words, to serve. When you go to a restaurant, a waiter or waitress comes to the table, gives you their name, informs you of the specials of the day, and asks to take your order. Their job is to wait on you and to serve you, to be attentive to you. They don't come to your table complaining about how bad of a day they've had or how frustrated they are. Nor do they lament about a customer who did not leave a tip. No! Their purpose is to serve, not be served.

Our purpose, just like Jesus', is to serve, or to minister. Ministry is meeting needs; it is feeding the hungry, clothing the naked, teaching, ushering, serving on the deacon board, singing in the choir. Wherever there is a need, there you will find the opportunity for ministry. All believers are called to minister. You may not have the title, but all Christians have been called to minister or serve. All of us have been called to wait on tables, to perform menial tasks. Tasks that you may think are insignificant or beneath your skill level. No matter how insignificant the task, if God assigns it to you, then it is significant. We serve God by serving each other. When we meet the needs of others, we are ministering to God (Matt. 25:40)!

CHAPTER ONE

My Journey

My first introduction to church was attending services with my grandmother at Lewis Chapel Baptist Church. I recall thinking how boring it was and that I could not wait to go to Grandma's house to eat homemade preserves, pound cake, and pick pecans from the pecan tree in the backyard.

One day while we were outside playing football, my mother called my brother and me into the house. She instructed us, "Wash up because we are going to church." "Going to church? It's almost night time," we responded in disbelief. You go to church in the morning, not at night, or so we thought. So my brother and I got dressed and went to church. What a strange church it was. There was loud music, loud singing, and loud people. My siblings and I were shocked! We had never experienced anything like it before.

Unbeknownst to us, we were attending a revival at a Pentecostal church. My mother went back each night and on the final night of the revival, she went to the altar and received what is called, the "Baptism in the Holy Ghost with the evidence of speaking in tongues." She was speaking a foreign language that made no sense to me. I could not understand what she was saying. It was unusual. I did not know what to say or how to respond. The next morning she tried to explain to my stepfather what happened and she began speaking in tongues. He did not know what to do or how to react to this transformation taking place in my mother. He thought she was having a seizure. After her born again experience, their relationship was never the same. She had entered the kingdom of light while he was still in the kingdom of darkness. My mother had a new agenda, mind set, priorities, and way of living. There would be no more partying, smoking, drinking or use of profanity. This is where the battle began.

Whenever you decide to live holy, the enemy becomes upset and will try to use any means necessary to hinder your growth in God. He used my stepfather. In the weeks and months subsequent to my mother's conversion, he did not have much to say, but when it was time to go to church, he would "perform!" Suddenly he began talking and asking all sorts of questions. This ritual occurred every time we headed for the door to go to church. My mother was determined to live for God, although living with my stepfather made it very tough, but everything was about to change.

One morning after a serious argument the night before, my stepfather threw my mother's clothes down the stairs and shouted, "Get out!" He backed up a U-haul truck to the garage and loaded it with our bikes and clothes. We left that day, numb and speechless. To this day, I don't know how or what to feel about what happened. I never hated him or disliked him. I only wished he had not treated my momma so badly. She is the best momma a son could have. Throwing us out of the house was probably the best thing he did for us. Finally, we could attend church in peace. We no longer had the big nice house and I no longer had my own room, but I had something far more precious and valuable. I had peace. What a precious commodity!

As I reflect on those turbulent years, I realized that I survived mentally and emotionally because of the Church. It was my heaven away from the hell at home. It was my oasis in the middle of a desert situation. It was a means of escape, if only for a brief time. It was a welcome break from the stress and pressure of home life. Church provided a loving surrogate family and caring friends. It was where I learned about God and developed my relationship with Him. Thank God for the ecclesia, the called out ones, the saints, yes, the Church. I believe that is why I continue to be so passionate about the Church, God's Body. Also, I am an advocate for members becoming actively involved in ministry. It was at Church, that God instilled purpose and a sense of destiny in me. This is what I desired for others. I want to help men and women know that God has a plan for their lives. Even in the unlikely places and situations of our lives, God can reveal His purpose for you. I would soon discover this to be true in my personal life.

After graduating from high school, I was awarded a Reserve Officers' Training Corps (ROTC) scholarship to attend college. I knew my mother could not afford to send me to school, so I applied for different military scholarships.

During my years at N.C. A&T, I grew by leaps and bounds. The Bible came alive to me. I was witnessing and seeing God change lives. Even my roommate, who considered himself God's gift to women, gave His life to the Lord and was spirit-filled. It was during this time, I believe, that God placed a heart for ministry in me and gave me the desire to work in full-time ministry. The church I attended was located near the college campus. Everyday at 12:00 noon I would walk to the church and join the "mothers" for noon day prayer. I loved just hanging around the church, doing odd jobs, trying to help out wherever and whenever I could.

Army ROTC gave me my first taste of serving. My senior year, I was appointed Operations Officer. I was responsible for providing weekly training assignments for ROTC cadets. It required planning, organizing and scheduling. I loved it! I looked forward to Thursday, because that was the day to put the plan in action. I would plan all week for one day; Thursday. It was so fulfilling and rewarding to see my plans on paper come to life. My appointment as Operations Officer boosted my self-esteem more than anything. I realized that I was good at something- administration. N.C. A&T was preparing me for a greater level of responsibility. Friendships and bonds were formed during those years that are still strong today. My years at A&T helped me establish a firmer foundation in the Word, but there was more to come.

After graduation, I went to Officer Basic Course at Fort Belvoir, VA. Once I completed the course, I returned to Fayetteville. I was at a crossroad in my life. I was a college graduate, but unemployed. I looked for work applying at different places. At one point, I was so desperate that I applied at McDonalds and was turned down. I was in the wilderness, the desert. It was a place of humbling, loneliness, and confusion, but it was where God wanted me to be. For the next six months I sought and prayed for God's direction. I told Him, "Whatever you want me to do, I am willing." God used those six months to burn selfish desires and habits out of me. I had never felt so close to Him than during that six-month journey through the wilderness. It was my personal garden of Gethsemane. Once I said, "Yes" with my heart and not only my lips, then God moved me to the next level.

One day during prayer, I sensed God telling me to move to Washington, D.C. I had no desire to go there, much less live in the place where some referred to as "Chocolate City", but I could not shake what I was sensing. Some time afterwards, I received a phone call from Eric, a college friend. He had accepted an offer from the National Security

Administration and had to relocate to the Washington, D.C. area, asking me if I wanted to join him. Nonchalantly, I replied, "sure." I told God, "If this is you, then you will have to provide the financial means for me to go." The day before we left, I received a check in the mail. This would be a major transition, but I sensed God saying, "Now is the time to shift."

Eric and I moved to the Nation's Capitol with a combination of anxiety and excitement. He worked for a federal government agency and I accepted a position with a temporary agency. While working for the agency, I met Keith who was a Christian. He invited me to his church, but I was attending another church at the time, so I was not really interested in attending his church. However, Keith was very persistent. The name of the church was Greater Mt. Calvary Holy Church, located in the inner city of Washington, D.C. My mother instilled in me the importance of joining a fellowship and becoming a faithful servant in the ministry. She taught by word and example, that part of serving God is serving in the church. So on the second Sunday in December of 1987, I joined Greater Mt. Calvary Holy Church.

After receiving the *"right hand of fellowship,"* I was eager to join a ministry. The following week, the pastor appointed me to the Deacon Board. Later, I joined the Cassette Ministry, the choir, and the Sunday School Department. These were areas of training for me. Working with those ministries taught me a great deal about serving. Soon, I was elevated to the position of Co-Chairman of the Deacon Board. I did not know at the time, but God was preparing me for a greater level of responsibility.

Pastor Owens was elevated to the position of Bishop and he needed more help than ever before. We began discussing the possibility of me becoming his assistant on a full time basis. I was honored, scared, excited, and nervous. My prayers were answered! It finally happened! In January 1994, I joined the staff of Greater Mt. Calvary Holy Church as the Administrative Assistant to the Senior Pastor. I was eager to begin my new assignment. In 1998, I was licensed as a minister of the gospel and appointed Dean of the Calvary Bible Institute (CBI). Initially, I did not want to accept the position, but Bishop Owens advised me that he could not think of another person to fill the position. So in addition to my responsibilities as administrative assistant, I was responsible for providing leadership to CBI.   In 1999, Bishop Owens felt I was ready for ordination. I was shocked at the remote possibility of being ordained when it had only been a year since I received my first license. In the Mount Calvary Holy Church of America, Inc., (MCHCA) organization, a licensed minister must serve a minimum of 2 years before he/she is considered for the next level of licensure, which is the evangelist license. Once an evangelist has served with that license for at least two years, he/she can submit an application for ordination. Ordination confirms that the minister has been properly trained to pastor as well as perform the sacraments of the church. I was honored that he thought I was ready for ordination. I could not believe it. I silently wondered, "Is this the same man that told me that I was not called to preach?" And now, he is suggesting that I receive my ordination. In May 1999, one year after receiving my first license, I am ordained an elder in the Mount Calvary Holy Church of America, Inc.

In 2000, Bishop Owens, together with his wife who serves as the Co-Pastor were traveling by airplane when they experienced turbulence caused by severe winds. Once the plane landed, Bishop Owens reflected on the experience and pondered in his mind, who would lead the church should he and Co-Pastor became incapacitated or even worse, die. Death is a subject not easily discussed, but it is a part of living. Great leaders realize that they will not live forever. If the work of the ministry is to continue, a plan of succession must be put in place. Many leaders die and, unfortunately, their ministry die with them because they did not train or invest in another person to continue what they had begun. Bishop Owens began to look over the many spiritual sons and daughters of the ministry to consider who he could groom and train to succeed him and Co-Pastor. Additionally, the ministry was growing rapidly and they needed someone to assist with the pastoral care of the congregation and someone to preside over the Sunday morning service when he and Co-Pastor were out of town.

While preparing to address the Board of Ministers, Bishop was in prayer consulting the Lord about this particular issue. The Lord's response to him was, "The person you are looking for is in your midst." Bishop inquired of the Lord, "Who?" The Lord responded, "Cedric." During the last meeting of the year for the Board of Ministers, Bishop Owens outlined his vision and goals for the upcoming year. He ended the meeting by telling the story of his experience on the plane and stated that he was appointing an Associate Pastor, the first in the history of the church. When he announced my name, the ministers exploded with a thunderous applause. I was in shock. I was speechless. I never imagined God honoring me with such a position. I realized everything I have experienced was preparing me to fulfill this role. I also recognize that my role is not to be served, but to serve. I am in this position to serve the senior pastors as well as the people of God. In addition to serving as the Associate Pastor, I am blessed to serve in significant roles of leadership as the 2nd Vice Bishop and Jurisdictional Bishop in Mt. Calvary Holy Church of America, Inc., and Dean of the Adjutant's Academy of the Joint College of Bishops. My elevation to positions of leadership would not have been possible without me following Jesus's example of picking up the towel of servanthood.

CHAPTER TWO

Servants are Doers

What does true servanthood look like? Where can we find a model or template of serving? In St. John 13, Jesus models for us true servant-hood. It is in this passage of scripture that Jesus provides valuable tips on serving with excellence.

When it comes to serving, God is more interested in your DOING than your TALKING. Don't get me wrong, talking is important. The word of God admonishes us to confess the word. Verse 4 states that Jesus rises from supper, takes off His robe and washes feet. He did not announce what He was about to do, He just got up and did it. In other words, servants are active. They are not lazy.

God condemns laziness. Another word for laziness is slothfulness, which according to the dictionary is defined as being **habitually lazy**. The book of Proverbs lists several scriptures that address laziness or slothfulness. Here are just a few.

- **Proverbs 12:24**

*The hand of the diligent shall bear rule: but the **slothful** shall be under tribute.*

- **Proverbs 15:19**

*The way of the **slothful** man is as an hedge of thorns: but the way of the righteous is made plain.*

- **Proverbs 19:24**

*A **slothful** man hideth his hand in his bosom, and will not so much as bring it to his mouth again.*

- **Proverbs 21:25**

*The desire of the **slothful** killeth him; for his hands refuse to labour.*

Jesus was not slothful, but active. He was a doer! He noticed an unmet need and addressed that need. Throughout His ministry, the sick were healed, the lame walked, the blind received their sight, and He even raised the dead. Acts 10:38 sums it up:

"When it comes to serving, God is more interested in your DOING than your TALKING."

"How God anointed Jesus of Nazareth with the Holy Ghost and with power: who went about **doing good**, and healing all that were oppressed of the devil; for God was with him" (emphasis added).

Servants are not only doers, but they are doers of GOOD! They are in the business of meeting the needs of others. Servants realize that they are NOT the problem, but the solution to the problem. Everyone is created to solve a problem or answer a question. The scripture says in Ephesians 2:10 (AMP),

> *"For we are God's* [own] *handiwork (*His workmanship*), recreated in Christ Jesus,* [born anew] *that we may do those good works which God predestined (planned beforehand) for us* [taking paths which He prepared ahead of time]*, that we should walk in them* [living the good life which He prearranged and made ready for us to live]*."*

The enemy of your soul would like for you to believe that you are the problem. No! God created you to be the solution to the problem! You are hired to work because you are solving a problem or problems for your employer. When you stop solving problems, you will stop working, because your employer will fire you! The more problems you solve, the more valuable you are to the company. Your salary is based upon the number of problems you solve and the complexity of those problems.

> "Servants realize that they are NOT the problem, but the solution to the problem."

Jesus noticed a problem, dirty feet. He decided to solve the problem. He washed their feet. We, too, have been called to "wash feet." No, we have not been called to announce it. We have been called to do it! God blesses us and the work of our hands when we do! Read the words of the psalmist,

> *"And he shall be like a tree planted by the rivers of water, that bringeth forth his fruit in his season; his leaf also shall not wither; and whatsoever he **doeth** shall prosper." Psalm 1:3*

The word, prosper, comes from a Hebrew word which means to accomplish what was intended. Notice, prosperity is the result when we do. It's not enough to have good intentions, but you must act on your intentions. Jesus did not talk about washing the disciples' feet; He actually did it! Make up your mind to accomplish what you intended to do. Some of you intend to go to school or back to school. Have you applied? Have you selected the courses? Others intend to lose weight. Have you started an exercise regimen? Have you changed your eating habits? Is your doing aligned with your intending? Do you have a plan of action? God is waiting to prosper you, but divine prosperity only comes as a result of godly activity.

It has been said that we judge others by what they do and judge ourselves by what we intended to do. It has also been said that the road to hell is paved with good intentions. Many people have great ideas and make wonderful resolutions, but they never act upon them. They make excuses why they are not able to do what they intended to do. The only one that can stop you is you!

Look at yourself in the mirror and repeat after me, no more excuses! Make the decision to become a doer of good!

CHAPTER THREE

Servants are Initiators

Servants are self-starters. They are go-getters. They are self-motivated. No one suggested to Jesus to wash feet. Sometimes God reveals a problem to you that others do not detect. You become upset and wonder why nothing is being done about it. Maybe you are the one who God has anointed to do something about it! Whenever you see a problem or a void in your church and it annoys you and frustrates you, maybe you are the solution to the problem. Martin Luther, the German theologian, strongly disagreed with the doctrine of the Catholic Church that forgiveness of sin could be purchased. Luther disputed this notion and wrote that only God could forgive sin and that faith in Jesus Christ was sufficient for salvation. These writings became known as the The 95 Thesis, which was the start of the protestant reformation. Luther was an initiator.

We have been called to solve problems. The enemy wants you to believe that you are the problem. On the contrary, you are the solution. You are the answer to the question. God has gifted you to be a solution, not a problem! There is something in you that God wants to use to bless your house, bless your church, bless your community, bless the world! Refuse to **"You have made mistakes, but you are not a mistake."** continue to believe the lie of Satan. The lie that says you are not good, you have nothing to offer, the lie that says you are a mistake. There are no mistakes in God. You have made mistakes, but YOU ARE NOT A MISTAKE. You are the apple of His eye! Take the initiative to resolve the problem. Meet with the leadership and ask how you can help solve the situation.

Matthew 25:14-17 (KJV)

14 For *the kingdom of heaven is* as a man travelling into a far country, *who* called his own servants, and delivered unto them his goods.

15 And unto one he gave five talents, to another two, and to another one; to every man according to his several ability; and straightway took his journey.

16 Then he that had received the five talents **went and traded with the same, and made *them* other five talents.**

17 And likewise he that *had received* two, he also gained other two.

Notice, the master did not tell the servant to invest the talents. He took the initiative to increase what was given to him. The word, traded, means to work, or to toil. God is a business man who expects a return on His investment. Since the beginning of time, He has commanded man to be fruitful and multiply (Genesis 1:28). Typically, when we read that scripture we think of bearing children. Although that is true, God is interested in you and me using our gifts and talents to help and serve others.

"The talent you possess is not for your benefit only, but it is to benefit your family, your friends, your congregation, even the world."

Just as God poured into you and me, we are called to pour into men, women, boys and girls. We are to reproduce God's gifts into those whom God has placed in our sphere of influence. The talent you possess is not for your benefit only, but it is to benefit your family, your friends, your congregation, even the world. Do not bury your gift, do not hide and say what you have to offer is insignificant. Somebody somewhere needs to hear what you have to say, needs to read what you have to write. Somebody somewhere is waiting for you to answer their question, to solve their problem. Start where you are; in your home, in your community, in your church, on your job. Trade with your talent; put it to work for the Kingdom and watch it increase for the Kingdom! Servants are initiators.

CHAPTER FOUR

Servants are Humble

"and [Jesus] laid aside His garments"

Humility is defined as willfully yielding. It is preferring others before yourself. Servants do not place the attention on themselves, but on others. Remember, to serve means to be attentive; attentive to the needs of others.

True humility does not produce pride, but it produces gratitude. It means you are not arrogant or haughty. Those types of persons are dependent upon themselves. They say, "look at what I have done," or "I did this," or "I did that." A humble person is dependent upon God. Servants who are humble say "God, if you don't help me, I won't be helped at all!" Humility is not belittling yourself or having a low opinion of yourself, but it is exalting and highly esteeming the God within you.

Humility is not weakness. As a matter of fact, a humble person is a powerful person. Humility is power under control. It requires more power to refrain from retaliation than to lash out when mistreated. Jesus says in John 10:17-18:

> *"Therefore doth my Father love me, because I lay down my life, that I might take it again. No man taketh it from me, but I lay it down of myself. I have <u>power</u> to lay it down, and I have <u>power</u> to take it again. This commandment have I received of my Father" (emphasis added).*

Humble people do not need to prove anything to anyone because their source is God. Humble people possess a healthy self-image because their image is based on the image that God has of them, not on the perceptions of man. The Bible says in Ephesians 2:10,

> *"For we are his workmanship , created in Christ Jesus unto good works, which God hath before ordained that we should walk in them."*

The scriptures further declare in Psalm 139:14:

> *"I will praise thee; for I am fearfully and wonderfully made: marvellous are thy works; and that my soul knoweth right well."*

Servants realize their value or worth is not based upon material possessions, their job, education, money, or people; it is based upon a personal relationship with the Heavenly Father. That is why Jesus was able to lay down his robe and put on a towel and wash feet. You see, during biblical times, one's garment signified one's status in the community. Jesus was known as a master teacher. He had "clout" in the community. Although He was respected as a master teacher, that was not the sum total of His identity. His identity, His self-worth was not based upon His occupation. He was secure enough within Himself to remove His robe, which represented His position and status, put on an apron, the symbol of a servant, and wash feet. Are you willing to humble yourself and remove your robe of status and replace it with an apron of servitude to meet the needs of others, or is your self-worth wrapped up and tied up in a position or title?

At the last supper, no servant was available to wash the disciples' feet when they entered the room. Everyone was around the table eating with dirty feet. No one wanted to handle the menial task of washing feet. It was beneath them, it was a duty reserved for the servant. But Jesus humbled Himself, got down and cleaned the dirt, grime and grit from the feet of the disciples. The master washed the feet of the servants. God is asking, are you willing to wash feet? In other words, are you willing to perform tasks, duties that no one is willing to perform? Are you available to serve people who are not in your circle, clique, or club? Can you wash the feet of someone who is different from you; someone of a different color, different background, different socio-economic level, or someone with less education than you?

> *Matthew 16:24(AMP)*
> *Then Jesus said to His disciples, If anyone desires to be My disciple, let him deny himself [disregard, lose sight of, and forget himself and his own interests] and take up his cross and follow Me [cleave steadfastly to Me, conform wholly to My example in living and, if need be, in dying, also].*

God is calling you and me to follow Christ's example of serving. He was willing to humble Himself, even to the point of death. Humility is willfully choosing to die to the desire of the flesh, whether it is your own flesh or the flesh of your friends, family, employer, etc. Death of fleshly desires must occur in order for the desires of the Heavenly Father to live and flourish. Carnal desires and Godly desires cannot co-exist. One has to die so that the other will live. Christ willfully chose to die so that the will of the Father would be manifested. Which will you chose?

"Carnal desires and Godly desires cannot co-exist. One has to die so that the other will live."

> *Philippians 2:5-9*
> *Let this mind be in you, which was also in Christ Jesus: Who, being in the form of God, thought it not robbery to be equal with God:*

But made himself of no reputation, and took upon him the form of a servant, and was made in the likeness of men:
And being found in fashion as a man, he humbled himself, and became obedient unto death, even the death of the cross.
Wherefore God also hath highly exalted him, and given him a name which is above every name:

Paul encourages us to adopt the same mindset as Christ. The Message Bible translation reads, "Think of yourselves the way Christ Jesus thought of himself." How did Christ think of Himself? He made Himself of no reputation. In other words, He did not exalt Himself or "toot His own horn." Although He had every right to do so, He did not boast and brag about being God. Instead, He chose to lower Himself and willfully become an obedient servant even to the point of obeying death. When you humble yourself before God, He will exalt you. He becomes responsible for your elevation. But when you exalt yourself or allow others to exalt you, then you will be brought to a low state (Luke 14:11). The word, exalt, means to elevate above others, to raise to the highest position. This level of promotion can only come from God, and only He can maintain it, not you.

In his book, *Good to Great*, Jim Collins lists the qualities that separate a good company from a great company. One of the qualities is a level 5 leader. Collins writes, "Level 5 leaders blend the paradoxical combination of personal humility with intense professional will. This rare combination also defies our assumption about what makes a great leader." Collins states that level 5 leaders realize that it is not about them, but about the company and the people they lead.

Leaders are servants who follow God. Paul said follow me as I follow Christ, (I Cor. 11:1). They submit to the will and way of God. Submit is defined as willfully yielding to someone or something. As stated earlier, Jesus willfully yielded to the Father's will by willfully yielding to death on a cross. Humility is the ability to submit even when you don't feel like submitting. It is saying yes when your flesh says no! And, sometimes, it is saying no when your flesh says go!

Occasions may arise when you want to go, but you must humble yourself and say no and stay in place. Jesus humbled Himself and went to the cross for you and I. He could have come down, but He remained in place. Legions of angels could have rescued Him, but He decided to stay that you and I might have everlasting life. And because He humbled Himself, God highly exalted Him. If you remain in place and serve with excellence, God will reward your service. Remember promotion does not come from man but from God. When God promotes you no one or no-thing can demote you.

CHAPTER FIVE

Servants Follow Through

Servants finish what they start. Jesus is our example. Notice in St. John 13, He rises from supper, He lays aside His garment, He girds himself with a towel, He pours water into a basin, He washes their feet, He dries their feet with the towel, puts back on His garment and sits down. He did not start and stop in the middle. He completed the process. He did not wash some of the feet and stop because he was tired. No! He finished what He started! Finish your God-given assignment, even if the conditions are against you.

> *Matthew 14:22-24*
> *And straightway Jesus constrained his disciples to get into a ship, and to go before him unto the other side, while he sent the multitudes away.*

And when he had sent the multitudes away, he went up into a mountain apart to pray: and when the evening was come, he was there alone. But the ship was now in the midst of the sea, tossed with waves: for the wind was contrary.

Jesus told the disciples to go to the other side. A storm arose that tried to prevent them from going to the other side. The scriptures say that the winds were contrary. The word contrary in the Greek language means opposing. Whenever Jesus gives you a command, you will face contrary or opposing winds; winds of doubt, winds of man's opinions, winds of insecurity, winds of lust and fleshly appetites. These and many others oppose us to stop us from fulfilling the will and purpose of God. No matter the severity of the storm, the

"No matter the severity of the storm, the command is go to the other side! The presence of contrary winds and storms is not an indication for you to stop."

command is go to the other side! The presence of contrary winds and storms is not an indication for you to stop. When the storm of adversity comes against you that is not the time to stop or quit. That is the time to persevere through the storm and follow through! God has given all believers an assignment. It is the job of Satan to prevent us from going to the other side, which prevent us from completing our God-ordained assignment. But remember, where God guides, God provides.

"Faithful is He who calleth you Who will also do it" (I Thes. 5:24).

Sometimes the contrary winds are disguised as small and insignificant tasks. No matter how menial or insignificant the tasks appear, follow through, finish what you start. Paul told Timothy, I have fought a good fight, **I have finished my course**, I have kept the faith (II Tim. 4:7). In other words, Paul was telling Timothy, I followed through. It was difficult at times, I did not understand everything God was doing, but I followed through. Yes! I was bored at times, frustrated and upset,

"When you make Jesus the center of your attraction, your activity or your attention, you can do the impossible."

but I followed through. In spite of trials and tribulations, follow through. Servants finish what they start: in other words, servants follow through.

Some of you may ask, "HOW do I follow through?" Let's look at our example, Jesus. Jesus teaches us how to follow through. Number 1, **maintain your focus**. Remember, you are on assignment from God; that is your purpose. Regardless of the distractions, Jesus maintained His focus. Focus is defined as the central point of attraction, activity or attention. Although storms are raging around you and within you, your point of attraction is not the storm. Your point of attraction is God and His purpose for your life.

Matthew 14:28-30
And Peter answered him and said, Lord, if it be
thou, bid me come unto thee on the water.
And he said, Come. And when Peter was come
down out of the ship, he walked on the water, to
go to Jesus.
But when he saw the wind boisterous, he was
afraid; and beginning to sink, he cried, saying,
Lord, save me.

Peter was focused on Jesus, and, as a result, he did the impossible! When you make Jesus the center of your attraction, your activity or your attention, you, too, can walk on water. You, too, can do the impossible. The impossible includes things that in and of yourself, you are incapable of doing. The impossible occurs when you step out of the boat of your comfort zone and step on the words that God spoke to you. The impossible is going to school because God said go and not because you have the tuition or because you are smart. The impossible is starting a ministry to help hurting and broken people when you have no financial resources. The impossible is defying human logic and reasoning and doing what God said, although you don't know the outcome. God is interested in performing what appears to be the impossible. Will you allow Him to perform the impossible through you? Maintain your focus!

When Peter stopped focusing on Jesus and focused on the wind, the thing he was walking on, he started sinking in. That which he had control over was now controlling him. Whatever has your attention has control. He exchanged the center of his attraction, activity and attention, who was Jesus, for the "boisterous winds." Another definition of focus is the state of maximum clarity of an image. Following through requires you to obtain and maintain a clear image of your purpose, of your assignment. Jesus had a very clear image or perspective of His purpose. He lived to die.

> *Matthew 16:21-23*
> *From that time forth began Jesus to shew unto his disciples, how that he must go unto Jerusalem, and suffer many things of the elders and chief priests and scribes, and be killed, and be raised again the third day.*
> *Then Peter took him, and began to rebuke him, saying, Be it far from thee, Lord: this shall not be unto thee.*
> *But he turned, and said unto Peter, Get thee behind me, Satan: thou art an offence unto me: for thou savourest not the things that be of God, but those that be of men.*

It was very clear to Jesus why He was born. He knew His destiny, and no-thing or no one was going to stop Him from completing His assignment, not even one of his closest friends. Don't allow friendships, and loved ones to stop you from completing your assignment. Satan will use anyone and anything to distract, deter, and detour you from your destiny. But you have to be determined "to go to the other side!" You must resolve in your mind and heart, like JESUS, that I will follow through by maintaining my focus. Jesus followed through all the way to Calvary.

He suffered physical, emotional pain, but He followed through to the cross. I am so glad He did! How about you!?

Secondly, **maintain your faith**. You maintain your faith by feeding your faith. The food for faith is the word of God.

> **Romans 10:17 (KJV)**
> 17 *So then faith cometh by hearing, and hearing by the word of God.*

Whatever you feed will grow. Man is a triune being. He is spirit, he has a soul, and he lives in a body. Soul is me-conscious; meaning that through the soul man is self-aware. It is in the soul where man discovers and determines likes and dislikes, strengths and weaknesses, joys and sorrows. The soul consists of the will, emotions and intellect. Then you have the body which is world-conscious. The body is man's connection with his surroundings. It is through the body that we experience the five senses; touch, taste, sight, hear, and smell.

We feed our soul through intellectual conversations, education, reasoning and rationality. The soul gains strength through "making sense" of the world outside as well as inside. People living on the soul realm live in a world where everything must have a logical reason for existing. We feed our body or flesh with natural food. Some foods are good and some are not so good. We also have fleshly appetites that are unhealthy. These appetites or lusts are a result of our sinful nature. When we give in to them, we are feeding our bodies. The scripture instructs us not to feed or fulfill the desires of our flesh, but to kill the deeds of the flesh (Romans 8:13; Colossians 3:5).

The spirit is God-conscious. God communicates with man initially through the spirit of man. The spirit is the REAL YOU. These three, spirit, soul, and body are the makeup of man. Each entity desires to control the other two. The one you feed will be the one that rules.

Your body is not you, it is the house in which you live. Just like your natural house is not you, it's a place where you reside. Genesis records that we are made in the image of God. John records that God is a body. No! John writes God is a spirit. Therefore, if we are made in the image or likeness of God and John writes God is a spirit, then it stands to reason that we are spirit. We feed the spirit with God's word. You, the spirit, become stronger and healthier by reading, studying, and meditating on the Word of God.

> **Psalm 1:2-3 (KJV)**
> *2 But his delight is in the law of the LORD; and in his law doth he meditate day and night.*
> *3 And he shall be like a tree planted by the rivers of water, that bringeth forth his fruit in his season; his leaf also shall not wither; and whatsoever he doeth shall prosper.*

Maintaining your faith requires you to feed your faith with a healthy portion of God's word. Jesus said Man shall not live by bread alone, but by every word that proceedeth out of the mouth of God. (Matthew 4:4). What He meant was that man cannot exist on natural food alone. If man is to live the life God has created him to live, the abundant life (John 10:10), then man must feed on the bread of life which is the word of God.

Lastly, **maintain your fight**. You and I are in a battle. The supervisor at your office or the person sitting next to you in worship service at church is not your enemy. People are influenced by the enemy to do mean things, but they are not the enemy. Satan is your enemy. The Bible states in 1 Peter 5:8 that Satan is our adversary. Although

> "We do not fight from a position of trying to gain the victory, we fight from the position that we have the victory."

he is our enemy, we must remember that he is a defeated enemy. He has lost the battle! We do not fight from a position of trying to gain the victory, we fight from the position that we have the victory! The fight is fixed! We have already won through the redemptive work of Jesus Christ!

2 Corinthians 2:14 (KJV)
14 Now thanks *be* unto God, which always causeth us to triumph in Christ, and maketh manifest the savour of his knowledge by us in every place.

God instructed the Israelites that He had given them the land of Canaan. It was a region flowing with milk & honey. In other words, it was a prosperous and fertile land. All Israel had to do was go in to Canaan and possess it. The book of Deuteronomy is filled with God reminding Israel to obey His commandments so that they could possess the land. Possessing the land meant they had to seize the land and dispossess those inhabiting the land. In other words, they had to fight for the territory God gave them. You and I must fight for our territory too! Our territory includes the assignment God gave us. Just like the assignment He gave the disciples to go to the other side. Enemies will attempt to stop you, the winds of adversity will blow against you, the Jebusites, Hitittes, Amorites, Perizzites, Hivites, and all the other "ites" will oppose you, but follow through. Maintain the fight against any and all foes that come to prevent you from possessing the promises of God. God has already secured your victory. All you and I must do is maintain our fighting stance! Here's how you do it.

As a believer, there are many weapons in your arsenal to defeat the enemy. The Bible tells us that the weapons of our warfare are not carnal but mighty through God. I will discuss these weapons in more detail in another chapter. But one weapon that is often overlooked is the weapon of obedience to God. The Bible states in James 4:7, "Submit yourself unto God, resist the devil and he will flee." Submit is defined as to come under in an orderly arrangement. Submission is voluntarily coming under another. If you are forced or coerced to do something then it is not submission. Another definition of submission is to obey. When you obey the voice of God you automatically defeat the enemy. Following through with God's instruction is certain to wreak havoc on the enemy. The Children of Israel defeated their enemies time and time again not because of their military prowess or because of great numbers. No! Because they obeyed God!

Deuteronomy 11:22-23 (KJV)
22 For if ye shall diligently keep all these commandments which I command you, to do them, to love the LORD your God, to walk in all his ways, and to cleave unto him;
23 Then will the LORD drive out all these nations from before you, and ye shall possess greater nations and mightier than yourselves.

Notice that God said, "IF" you do, "THEN" I will do. If you obey then I will drive out the enemy. It does not matter if the enemy is stronger or larger. You and God are the majority! Israel faced nations that were stronger, but God makes the difference in any battle! The scripture says that the LORD will drive out all the nations. In other words, God will dispossess the nations from the milk and honey land and allow you to possess the land they once occupied. Obedience to God secures your victory!

Gideon defeated the Midianites because he obeyed God by decreasing his army from 32,000 to 300. The walls of Jericho fell flat and the inhabitants were completely destroyed because Joshua and the children of Israel obeyed God by marching around the walls once a day for six days and seven times on the seventh day. Jehoshaphat led Israel to victory over three armies because they followed the Lord's instruction in II Chronicles 20 and did not fight but lifted up praises to God.

Finish what you started. God will help you follow through. Remember to maintain your focus, your faith, and your fight. Then you will be able to say, like Paul, "I finished my course!"

CHAPTER SIX

Servants Serve in Unfavorable Conditions

Jesus washed the disciples' feet knowing that He would soon receive 39 lashes from a cat-o-nine tails. Jesus washed the disciples' feet knowing that very soon a crown of thorns would be placed on His head. In spite of the suffering He was about to endure, Jesus washed feet. We, on the other hand, get a headache and cannot serve. Someone says something negative about us, and we don't want to come back to church. Jesus knew that soon He would carry a cross to Golgotha Hill. In the midst of all that, He took off His garments, girded himself with a towel, and washed feet. Sometimes we feel we need someone to wash our feet. God never said that serving would be easy. But He did promise that He would be by our side. Although you are consumed with problems, God gives you grace to minister to others who are in need. When you are attentive to the needs of others, God is attentive to your needs. Whatever you make happen for someone else, God will make happen for you! Paul asked God three times to remove the thorn from his flesh. God's response was, "My grace is sufficient" (II Cor. 12:9). In other words, you can still do what I called you to do even though the conditions, externally and internally, are not comfortable. You see, there are things happening around us and within us that may not be the best of circumstances. Regardless, God has not changed His mind about your call to servanthood. Although you have asked Him repeatedly to remove "it" or "him" or "her" and He hasn't, that is not an indication for you to stop serving. God's response, God's remedy for your malady is grace; His unmerited favor upon you which empowers you to do what you cannot do. Child of God, His grace is all you need. Through His grace, you can serve faithfully and joyfully.

"Although you are consumed with problems, God gives you grace to minister to others who are in need."

"Grace is God's Resources Available in Chaotic Events."

Grace for the Race

The Christian life is equated to a race. Everyone has a lane assignment. Your assignment is different from mine. In a race, the course is already set. The runner does not have to wonder which direction to run. All the runner has to do is run the pre-determined course. You and I have a pre-determined course to run. The Bible says in **Hebrews 12:1,** "Wherefore seeing we also are compassed about with so great a cloud of witnesses, let us lay aside every weight, and the sin which doth so easily beset *us, **and let us run with patience the race that is set before us***" (emphasis added). God has set the course for your life. Furthermore, He has empowered and equipped you to successfully complete the course. Everything you need to run the race, God has graced you with it. Pastor, you are well able to lead that congregation. Ministry leader, God has equipped you to handle the challenges that come with leading people to accomplish objectives and goals. Husband, you can become the leader of your home that God has called you to become. It does not matter what your calling, vocation, or occupation is, God's grace is sufficient.

CHAPTER SEVEN

Servants Serve Unfavorable People

G od did not say that serving others would be an easy task. Jesus is our model. Scripture states He washed the disciples' feet. He washed all twelve sets of feet, including Judas, the one who betrayed Him. Jesus knew that Judas would betray Him as He got on His knees to wash his feet. He washed Peter's feet knowing that Peter would deny Him three times. Jesus washed the disciples' feet knowing they would desert Him. Jesus served the disciples in spite of their mistreatment of Him. You and I are called to serve those who treat us unfavorably. It is easy to serve people who are courteous, nice, and appreciative. But can you serve people who do not like you? Can you help those who mistreat you and are unappreciative? Do you serve only the people who like you? If you do, so what!? God is not impressed. God is impressed when you wash the feet of those who act unfavorably toward you. God wants us to serve one another even if the person you are serving is rude or inconsiderate.

Luke 6:32-35 (KJV)

32 For if ye love them which love you, what thank have ye? for sinners also love those that love them.

33 And if ye do good to them which do good to you, what thank have ye? for sinners also do even the same.

34 And if ye lend to them of whom ye hope to receive, what thank have ye? for sinners also lend to sinners, to receive as much again.

35 But love ye your enemies, and do good, and lend, hoping for nothing again; and your reward shall be great, and ye shall be the children of the Highest: for he is kind unto the unthankful and to the evil.

Servants are God's representatives in the earth realm. We are ambassadorsof the Kingdom of God. Therefore our actions should reflect the God we represent. Pastor Jentezen Franklin said, "Your conduct should match your context." What he means is that your actions should be a reflection of who you are and where you are in your life's journey. For example, if your context is single, then your conduct or your actions should not be that of someone who is married. There are several single men and women

> "God expects you and me to serve even when the behavior of one we are serving is unfavorable."

who are having sex and living together as if they are married, but they are not. Then you have husbands and wives who are conducting themselves as if they are single. Not accountable to their spouse, spend too much time with single friends. Our context as servants should be reflected in our conduct toward others; even if they mistreat us, don't speak to us and take advantage of us. Jesus exemplifies servanthood by washing the disciples' feet with the knowledge that Judas would betray Him. Jesus washed feet knowing that the disciples would desert Him. Jesus served humanity by sacrificing His life, knowing that all of humanity would not accept Him as Lord and Savior. They spat on Him, but He served. They placed a crown of thorns on His head, but He still served. They beat Him all night long, yet He served them. He had the power to remove Himself from all of this, but instead, He used His power to serve! What a mighty God we serve!

CHAPTER EIGHT

The Spirit of an Armor Bearer

I believe that everyone who serves in ministry should possess the spirit of an armor bearer. Let me explain. The term, **Armor bearer,** is translated from two Hebrew words:

> **Nacah** (naw-saw') – *Means to lift. Some applications are to accept, advance, bear up, and to carry away.*
>
> **Keliy** (Kel-ee') – *Means to end. Some of the applications are to complete, consume, destroy utterly, and to finish.*

Therefore, the definition of an __armor bearer__ is a *person who ends, consumes, or utterly destroys the attacks of the enemy by lifting, bearing up or carrying away a particular load or burden from the leader.*

A load is any responsibility within the ministry. It can range from ushering at the door to working in children's ministry to handling the sound to counting the offering. If you are responsible for overseeing any of those areas or one of the many other areas of ministry, then you are an armor bearer. It is more than carrying a pastor or leader's Bible or briefcase. It is lifting a load or responsibility of the ministry so that the leader does not have to focus on that area. He or she can focus on their calling, feeding the flock of God. There is a great example of this in the book of Exodus.

> *(Exodus 17:9-13)*
>
> *And Moses said unto Joshua, Choose us out men, and go out, fight with Amalek: to morrow I will stand on the top of the hill with the rod of God in mine hand.*
> *So Joshua did as Moses had said to him, and fought with Amalek: and Moses, Aaron, and Hur went up to the top of the hill.*
> *And it came to pass, when Moses held up his hand, that Israel prevailed: and when he let down his hand, Amalek prevailed.*
> *But Moses' hands were heavy; and they took a stone, and put it under him, and he sat thereon; and Aaron and Hur stayed up his hands, the one on the one side, and the other on the other side; and his hands were steady until the going down*

of the sun. And Joshua discomfited Amalek and his people with the edge of the sword.

From these verses we observe a few things about armor bearing.

One does not have to work closely with the Pastor/leader to be an armor bearer.

When you read the scripture, Joshua is not near Moses, however, he is an armor bearer. Why? Because he is ending, consuming, or utterly destroying the attack of the enemy by lifting, bearing up or carrying away a particular load or burden from the leader. In this case, the load he is carrying is the load of fighting the Amalekites. Therefore, Moses does not have to.

> "One does not have to work closely with the Pastor/leader to be an armor bearer."

Remember, a load is any aspect of the ministry. It could be ushering, media ministry, deacon's ministry, finance ministry, outreach ministry, music ministry, etc. If you are working in any aspect of ministry, you are carrying a load that the pastor/leader does not have to carry. They are able to focus on the "load" that God called them to bear, leading and preaching to the congregation.

Armor bearers are not jealous, covetous, or envious of one another.

Nowhere in scripture do we read Aaron, Hur and Joshua were envious or coveted the position of the other. Envy is defined as longing to possess something awarded to or achieved by another. Jealousy is a feeling of resentment that another has gained something that one more rightfully deserves. To covet is to desire wrongfully, inordinately, or without due regard for the property or rights of others. They served where they were assigned. I imagine they realized that they were on the same team. Armor bearers are more concerned about accomplishing the mission than they are about obtaining a position. They know that teamwork makes the dream work.

> "Armor bearers are called to complement the leader, not compete with the leader."

Don't covet a person's position, status or relationship with the pastor/leader. God has an assignment for everybody. Find where you fit and go to work! True fulfillment comes from fulfilling God's will, not your will. When we find our fit then together we can accomplish so much for the Kingdom of God. As the saying goes, "Where there's unity, there's strength."

In Genesis, the people of Babel attempted to build a tower to heaven. These people were heathens, in other words, they did not acknowledge or serve God. The Bible states that God came down to see what they were doing. His assessment is recorded in chapter 11 and verse 6.

"And the Lord said, Behold, the people is one, and they have all one language; and this they begin to do: and now nothing will be restrained from them, which they have imagined to do."

God said the people "is" one. The word "is" denotes singular not plural. The word, people, is a plural noun. But the scriptures record that the people is one! The Babel people were so unified that God saw them as one cohesive unit. He also said that *"nothing will be restrained from them which they imagine to do."* Restrained means fenced in, isolated, inaccessible. In other words because they were so unified, nothing will be fenced in, isolated or inaccessible to them. Now remember these people were not Christians, they were not disciples; but God said nothing will be withheld from them. Now if God said this about ungodly people, imagine what you and I, as Godly people, can accomplish, if we worked in unity. Imagine the projects, which seem impossible, we could accomplish if we only unite our gifts, talents, and skill sets. We are many members but one body. I need your gifts, talents and skills, and you need mine. In his book, *In Search of Timothy*, Tony Cooke writes that we are "deficient by design." He continues, *"God deliberately made me deficient. The gifts He didn't give to me, He may have given to you. The only way the local church can be successful is for us to recognize that we are individually deficient by design, to honor and respect the gifts He's given others, and finally to use them together-in partnership and teamwork-for the building up of the Kingdom."*

Armor bearers are not jealous, covetous, or envious of the Pastor/leader.

Armor bearers are called to complement the leader, not compete with the leader. We are called to help the pastor/leader succeed in accomplishing the mission God has given them. Do not allow a spirit of envy or covetousness to cloud your judgment or affect your level and quality of service. Even when the leader is upset with you, do not allow your emotions to get the best of you. Don't leave your assignment. Stay right there and continue to serve with excellence.

Ecclesiastes 10:4 (KJV)
4 If the spirit of the ruler rise up against thee, leave not thy place; for yielding pacifieth great offences.

This scripture reminds me of a situation that occurred at my church, Greater Mt. Calvary Holy Church. During this time, I served as Bishop Alfred Owens' administrative assistant. I also assisted him in the pulpit. The church had just completed refurbishing a warehouse and converted it into a food and clothing bank. It was one of Bishop's visions that had come to fruition. The food bank was a modern-day grocery store with aisles of food. People from the community could come and pick up food at no cost! Bishop was so excited. The keys to the food bank were given to him, which he gave to me. I put the keys in my pocket and thought no more about it. When I went home that evening, I placed the keys on my dresser. During our Sunday morning worship service, Bishop whispered to me that he would like to open the Food bank and allow the congregation to see what the Lord had done! He asked me, "Where are the keys?" I responded, "At home." The look on his face said it all. Now, remember we are in the pulpit in front of 2000 people. He says to me with a look of disgust, "Why are the keys at home?!" He said it three times. Then he said, "Go home, Cedric, and get the keys!" Guess how many times he said it? You're right, three times. So what did I do? I went home, which was a 20-minute drive, in my robe, and got the keys.

Driving home, I was upset, embarrassed, and humiliated. I did not want to go back to church, but I did. I returned to the pulpit and I whispered to him, "Bishop, I have the keys." He responded with irritation, "Thank you!" I had a choice to make. Either I was going to sit there and sulk, be depressed, upset or I was going to get up and praise and worship the Lord along with the congregation and Bishop Owens! I chose the latter. Although I wanted to leave my post, I didn't. Sometimes you will feel embarrassed, wrongly accused, overlooked, under appreciated by your leader. Solomon said in Ecclesiastes, don't leave your post. God has empowered and equipped you to handle tough times and tough moments.

Remember what you make happen for your leader, God will make happen for you. Your level of sowing into your leader will determine your level of reaping from God. If you continue to sow seeds of service even in the midst of adversity, you will reap a bountiful harvest!

Armor bearers help "stay" the hands of the Pastor/leader.

Stayed is defined as to hold up; to provide **support** or to gird up. Support is defined as to maintain in position so as to keep from falling, sinking, or slipping; to keep from failing or yielding during stress. In scripture, the hand symbolizes power, work, and ministry. Therefore armor bearers hold up and maintain his or her position in order that the hands or the ministry doesn't fall, sink, or slip. Dr. Samuel Chand states in his book, "*Who's Holding Your Ladder?*", that the higher a leader climbs the ladder of ministry, the more ladder holders he or she needs at the base of the ladder. Armor bearers are the main supporters of the work of the ministry. Pastors/leaders need people who will support the vision with passion and excellence. The vision is always larger than the visionary. God gives the leader a vision that that he or she cannot execute alone. Look at it from the natural perspective. You have the ability to see more than what you can physically handle. Look around a room; you see all the contents of the room, but you cannot handle all the contents alone. When God gives a pastor/leader a vision, He never expects the leader to fulfill the vision alone. Where there's vision, there's PROvision. God connects followers to leaders to help leaders fulfill the vision. The scripture records that as long as Moses' hands were up, Joshua and Israel prevailed. When Moses' hands became tired, Aaron and Hur held them up. Moses, Aaron, Hur and Joshua were all connected so that victory could be won. No one obtains victory alone. It is a team effort. Because Aaron and Hur stayed, or supported, Moses's hands, Joshua and the Israelites prevailed. Armor bearers, support your man or woman of God so that the ministry will prevail against the enemy.

Armor bearers help "steady" the hands of the Pastor/leader.

Because Aaron and Hur stayed the hands of the Moses, his hands were steady. Armor bearers are a key to the success of the ministry becoming "steady". **Steady** is defined as stable, established, faithful, reliable, dependable, constancy of character or purpose. The ministry is as reliable as the people who make up the ministry. If the ministry is perceived as unstable, unreliable, undependable, it is because the people are perceived in that manner. Steady people equal steady ministry.

"Ask yourself, am I an asset or a liability to the ministry?"

Leaders must be men and women who are constant in character. They must be men and women of integrity. Armor bearers must follow suit.

Leaders need followers who will maintain a standard of righteousness and moral character; men and women who are committed to live a life according to God's word. Reliable armor bearers are punctual and ready to serve when they arrive. They handle the business of their leader even when things are not ideal in their own lives. Ask yourself these questions, Can the pastor/leader depend on me? Am I profitable to the ministry (II Tim. 4:11; Philemon 1:11)? The word profitable comes from the Greek word, euchrestos (yoo'-khrays-tos), which is defined as easily used or useful. Here are a few more questions for you. Am I useful, easily used or am I difficult to use? Do I make excuses when it comes to serving? Do I serve only when I feel like it or when things are going well for me? Am I an asset or a liability to the ministry?

CHAPTER NINE

Qualifications of an Armor Bearer, Part I

T he Bible lists several characteristics of an armor bearer. Let's take a look at them.

>*And Saul said unto his servants, Provide me now a man that can play well, and bring him to me.Then answered one of the servants, and said, Behold, I have seen a son of Jesse the Bethlehemite, that is cunning in playing, and a mighty valiant man, and a man of war, and prudent in matters, and a comely person, and the LORD is with him. And David came to Saul, and stood before him: and he loved him greatly; and he became his armourbearer. (I Samuel 16:17-18, 21)*

King Saul sought for a man that could play a musical instrument well. He wanted someone who had the ability to effectively minister to him. One of his servants spoke up and said he had seen someone who was capable of fulfilling the king's request. His name was David. Then the servant lists six qualities he had observed in David. I am certain that David was not aware that this young servant was observing him. Who observes shepherd boys? All they do is feed sheep and clean up after

"Your performance today will determine your promotion tomorrow."

them, clean them and protect them from predators. David was performing what seems to be menial tasks; nothing of significance or importance. Right? Wrong! You never know who is observing you. That's why it is so important that you perform your assignment with excellence no matter how small or insignificant it seems to you or others. Someone is watching! Your performance today will determine your promotion tomorrow.

> *Matthew 25:21 (KJV)*
> *21 His lord said unto him, Well done, thou good and faithful servant: thou hast been faithful over a few things, I will make thee ruler over many things: enter thou into the joy of thy lord.*

One day David is in the field with sheep and the next he is in the palace with the king. How did he do it!? Let's take a look.

I. Cunning in playing

The servant said David was cunning in playing. At first glance the word cunning has a negative meaning; sly, deceptive. In this context, cunning is defined as skillful, competent, knowledgeable and resourceful. Effective armor bearers are well-versed and skillful in serving within their assignment. Never feel you know all there is to know about your area of service. Constantly seek out new materials, talk to people who you consider experts in your area; read books and articles, attend workshops/seminars, or enroll in a course. It is not enough to be anointed. Now, don't get me wrong, anointing is vital to your assignment. But acquiring more knowledge and expertise about your ministry through reading or taking a course will make you that much more effective!

II. A mighty valiant man.

Secondly, the servant said David is a mighty valiant man. In other words, David is a man of courage. Courage is the ability to handle opposition, adverse circumstances and difficult situations in the midst of fear. It is also defined as firmness of mind and will in the face of danger or extreme difficulty; mental strength to venture, persevere, and withstand danger, fear, or difficulty.

Anyone can act valiantly when things are going their way. But how do you perform when it seems everything and everyone is against you? It takes courage to move forward when you feel afraid or intimidated. There are times you have to do it afraid. Some of you may ask, what do you mean? Well, every assignment given to you will not always agree with you. Some assignments may appear to be intimidating or even overwhelming, but remember you are well able to perform. Therefore, you may have to perform the task feeling afraid. Don't allow your fear to stop you. Do it even in midst of fear, do it afraid. Do it and watch God show up and show out! 1 Thessalonians 5:24 states, "**Faithful is he that calleth you, who also will do it.**"

You did not call yourself to the assignment, God did! If He called you TO it, then God will DO it, through you! Moses did not choose himself to deliver the Children of Israel from Egypt, God chose him (Exodus 3:10). God knew Moses's strengths and weaknesses before He selected Moses. He did not make a mistake. Moses was not selected based upon his ability. God does need not your ability; he wants your availability. God has all the ability or power needed to get the job done. He is looking for a willing vessel that will say, "Here am I, send me!" When Moses went off the scene, God turned to Joshua and said,

> **5 There shall not any man be able to stand before thee all the days of thy life: as I was with Moses, so I will be with thee: I will not fail thee, nor forsake thee.**
> **6 Be strong and of a good courage: for unto this people shalt thou divide for an inheritance the**

"If He called you TO it, then God will DO it, through you!"

land, which I sware unto their fathers to give them.
Joshua 1:5-6

You can have courage or firmness of mind because God is with you! He will not fail you nor forsake you. When others give up and give out on you, God is a constant and consistent support. You can always trust Him to come through for you.

III.   A Man of War

David was not only a skillful musician, but he was a skillful warrior. He was an experienced fighter. He fought and defeated a bear, a lion and Goliath! When David became king, he transformed a nation of farmers to a nation of soldiers. Servants must become skillful in the art of combat. I am referring to spiritual combat. Ephesians 6:12 states, "For we wrestle not against flesh and blood, but against principalities, against powers, against the rulers of the darkness of this world, against spiritual wickedness in high places." The believers are in a battle, whether they know it or not. We are in a spiritual battle and must be combat-ready. Let me explain. I grew up near one of the largest military bases in the world, Fort Bragg, NC. From my house, I could hear troops performing training exercises. Occasionally, I would see paratroopers falling from the sky as they jumped out of planes. The training was for preparation in the event they had to be deployed to a battlefield somewhere in the world. They could not start preparing when they received the call; they had to be ready to go at a moment's notice. As it is in the natural, so it is in the spirit. We are in a spiritual battle and must be "combat-ready". Let me explain. If you receive a call that the leader is under attack, you can't get ready to enter warfare, you should be ready to do battle against the forces of darkness.

As a college student at North Carolina A&T State University, I was a cadet in Army ROTC program. We learned how to fire a M-16 rifle, how to lead a squad, platoon, company, and a battalion. We learned about teamwork and operating as a cohesive unit. We also learned how to engage in combat. The instructors taught us that to be effective in combat you had to know the Rules of War. Well, I have come up with a few "Rules of War" for the spiritual battle.

Rule of War #1 - Know your Enemies

Men and women of war are clear about the enemies of their soul. Unfortunately, many of us believe our supervisor on the job is the enemy, or the person in the cubicle next to you is the enemy. Some believe the enemy is the neighbor next door or down the street. We have mistaken our brother or sister in Christ as our enemy. The Bible clearly points out the enemies of the believer. Let's examine each one.

> *1 Peter 5:8 (KJV)*
> *8 Be sober, be vigilant; because your adversary the devil, as a roaring lion, walketh about, seeking whom he may devour:*

Satan is an enemy to the believer. It is his "mission in life" to stop, impede, hinder, destroy, distract, detain, disrupt and detour you from fulfilling the destiny God has for your life. He desires you so that he may, as Jesus states, "sift you as wheat" (Luke 22:31). Sifting is the process of separating small particles from larger particles by placing them in a sifter or sieve. In the original Greek language, the word, sift, means to scatter. Satan desires you, he lusts after you so that he may break you down and separate and scatter you. He wants to confuse you, he wants you to become so mixed up and messed up that you are no threat to him and no good for the Kingdom of God. The good news is that Satan is defeated. His destiny is set and he cannot change it. Christ defeated Satan on the cross. Because we are joint heirs with Christ, we have victory over Satan and his tactics, schemes, weapons and tricks. Jesus reminds us in St. Matthew 16:18 that the gates of hell will not prevail against the church. Job reminds us that he (Satan) is limited. Satan is:

> "Satan is limited in presence, power, knowledge and authority."

Limited in presence – Job 1:7
Limited in power – Job 1:10
Limited in knowledge – Job 1:11& 22
Limited in authority – Job 1:12

Another enemy of the believer is the world. I John 2:15 states, "Love not the world, neither the things that are in the world. If any man loves the world, the love of the

Father is not in him." The definition of the word, world, is the orderly arrangement or the way of doing things. So the message the scripture is conveying is do not love the world's way of doing things. We are in the world but not of the world. We do not follow the customs and traditions of this world. We are citizens of a different kingdom, the Kingdom of God.

> "Do not love the world's way of doing things."

Finally, your carnal mind is your enemy. The carnal mind is when you allow fleshly desires to control you. It is giving in to the lust of the flesh, the lust of the eye and the pride of life. The flesh or the carnal mind does not desire to fulfill the plan of God. As a matter of fact the Bible lets us know that the carnal mind is enmity or hostile towards God.

Romans 8:6-8 (KJV)
6 For to be carnally minded *is* death; but to be spiritually minded *is* life and peace.
7 Because the carnal mind *is* enmity against God: for it is not subject to the law of God, neither indeed can be.
8 So then they that are in the flesh cannot please God.

Rule of War #2 - Know your weapons (II Corinthians 10:3-4)

Effective fighters are knowledgeable of the weapons at their disposal. They know which type will work best in the current situation. As spiritual warriors, we must be knowledgeable of the weapons in our arsenal.

The Word of God

When Jesus entered the wilderness, the devil asked Him a series of questions. Each time His response was, "It is written", St. Matthew 4:1-11. Jesus did not fight Satan with His intellect, His emotions, or with His own words. No! He used the weapon of God's Word. We must utilize the Word of God appropriately. It is not enough to memorize scripture, but we must know when to use it. That is why Paul admonishes the believer to "Study to shew thyself approved unto God, a workman that needeth not to be ashamed, rightly dividing the word of truth" (II Tim 2:15).

In the book of Ephesians, Paul lists the spiritual armor of the believer. Included in that list is the only offensive weapon, the Word of God.

Ephesians 6:17 (KJV)
17 And take the helmet of salvation, and the sword of the Spirit, which is the word of God:

Praise

Praise is to Satan what kryptonite is to Superman. Praise weakens Satan. Praise muffles the sound of the enemy. It is amazing that while you are praising God, at the same time you are stifling the enemy (Psalm 8:2). While you are lifting up God, you are tearing down the enemy. Praise is multifaceted. "Many" things happen

"Praise is to Satan what kryptonite is to Superman."

when you do the "one" thing (Acts 16:23-26). In II Chronicles 20:22 we see clearly the weapon of praise actively engaged.

Where does God hang out? Where does He live? What is His address? His address is praise!

Psalm 22:3 (KJV)
3 But thou art holy, O thou that inhabitest the praises of Israel.

The word, inhabitest is defined as to sit down, to dwell, to settle. God lives, dwells, will sit down in the midst of your praises. If you want to attract God to your situations and problems, begin praising Him! Inhabitest also means to marry. God is married to, joined to, your praise.

"Praise is God's address."

The Name of Jesus.

You and I have been granted the powerful privilege to use the name of Jesus. When we say, "In the Name of Jesus!" it is as if He is doing it. We have been granted power of attorney to use the name of Jesus Christ. In other words, we can conduct business on His behalf. So Satan has to back up when we say, "In Jesus' Name!"

> **Mark 16:17-18 (KJV)**
> 17 And these signs shall follow them that believe; In my name shall they cast out devils; they shall speak with new tongues;

18 They shall take up serpents; and if they drink any deadly thing, it shall not hurt them; they shall lay hands on the sick, and they shall recover.

Rule of War #3 - Know your Ally (God is your ally)

You and God are the majority!

Isaiah 41:10 (KJV)
10 Fear thou not; for I *am* with thee: be not dismayed; for I *am* thy God: I will strengthen thee; yea, I will help thee; yea, I will uphold thee with the right hand of my righteousness.

No need to worry or be anxious. God is WITH you. The word "with" has two meanings. The first is to accompany someone as a companion or as a partner. God is your companion or partner. You and God are in business together as partners. The business is His will. You never have to be concerned about God as your partner. He will always hold up His end of the deal. Not only will God hold up His end, but He will empower you to hold up your end. You cannot do it in your strength anyhow!

1 Thessalonians 5:24 (KJV)
24 Faithful is he that calleth you, who also will do it.

Listen, if God called you to it, then He's equipped you to perform it. God is by your side. He said I will never leave you nor forsake you. Rest assured that God is with you. He has decided to co-labor with you. You and God are partners. If you have the availability, God has the ability! That's why He sent His Holy Spirit in to your life, to help you, to empower you to effectively execute His purpose and plan!

> *"So, God is not only by your side, but He is also on your side!"*

> **Acts 1:8 (AMP)**
> **8 But you shall receive power (ability, efficiency, and might) when the Holy Spirit has come upon you, and you shall be My witnesses in Jerusalem and all Judea and Samaria and to the ends (the very bounds) of the earth.**

The second definition of with: to be "supportive of". So, God is not only *by* your side, but He is also *on* your side! God is your biggest fan, God is your biggest cheerleader. Look at what the psalmist writes about God's attitude toward man.

> **Psalm 8:4-6 (KJV)**
> **4 What is man, that thou art mindful of him? and the son of man, that thou visitest him?**
> **5 For thou hast made him a little lower than the angels, and hast crowned him with glory and honour.**

6 Thou madest him to have dominion over the works of thy hands; thou hast put all things under his feet:

God is all about helping you succeed. If you set your eyes on Him, you will not fail (Psalm 16:8).

IV. Prudent in matters.

In other words, David was wise in practical affairs. He was confidential and trustworthy. He knew when to speak and when to be quiet. David had the ability to handle sensitive issues and information. As a servant, as an armor bearer, you will have the privilege of knowing sensitive information. Because of your position, you may have knowledge of issues that others will not have. You have to know it and not talk about it. People will ask you for information. But you must be "prudent" in matters, like David. Listen, just because you know it doesn't mean you have to tell it! Can you be trusted with information about other people and not become adversely affected by the information or have a negative attitude toward them? Are you able to handle the pressure of knowing something, even if it is about your leader, and not allow it to affect how you serve God and your leader? David was able to do it.

The Bible records in I Samuel 18 Saul throws a javelin at David while he is ministering to Saul. David avoids being hit by the javelin. This occurred twice! David did not retaliate nor talked negatively about Saul, at least it's not recorded in scripture. Despite Saul's attempt to kill him,

David fought and won many battles for Saul. Verse 14 states, "and David behaved himself wisely in all his ways." In chapter 18, we also read that Saul offered his eldest daughter, Merab (whose name means increase) to David. When it was time for the wedding, it was discovered that she was married to another man. So Saul offered to David his other daughter, Michal (whose name means small brook). So David went from "increase" to a "small brook." But in order for David to marry Michal, he had to bring Saul the foreskins of 100 Philistines. Saul was hoping that David would be killed in the midst of the battle against the Philistines. David returns with 200 foreskins!

I believe David knew that he was in that position not because of Saul, but because of God. His service was not based on Saul's action or reaction, but based on God's assignment for his life. Although Saul hated David and made many attempts to kill him, David did not retaliate nor did he disrespect or slander the king. Can the same be said of you?

V.   A comely person.

The word, comely, means attractive or handsome. David was a handsome young man. He was not only physically attractive, but David had an attractive disposition and personality.   The Bible says Saul loved him, Jonathan's soul was knitted to him. The women sang a song about his exploits in battle. The people and even Saul's servants approved of him.

1 Samuel 18:5 (MSG)
5 Whatever Saul gave David to do, he did it—and did it well. So well that Saul put him in charge of his military operations. Everybody, both the people in general and Saul's servants, approved of and admired David's leadership.

People were drawn to David probably because he was friendly, approachable and not high-minded. David realized that he was not only Saul's servant, but a servant to the people. Please remember that you are called to serve not only your leader, but the people as well. Don't become so consumed with your position that you become arrogant and believe that you are better than the people you are called to serve. Don't mistreat and mishandle God's precious saints. You're not all that! Remain approachable, friendly and humble. Remember it is by God's grace, not your ability that you are in that position. Remember as armor bearers, as adjutants, as ministry leaders we are in the people business. We are called to minister to the people, not be ministered to by the people! If you do not like people, you're in the wrong business. Yes, it's nice to be comely in appearance, but it's nicer to be comely in attitude. Examine yourself and determine if your attitude attracts or repel the people of God. If it's the latter, then ask God to help you change.

VI.   The Lord is with him.

In other words, David was anointed by God. If I had to choose one reason why David was so successful this would be the reason. The anointing is God superimposing His ability over your ability so that you can successfully perform what He has assigned to you. I like to say it is God placing "super" on your "natural." The word, anoint means to rub or smear oil on something or someone. When God anoints something or someone, He smears His presence, His power on it or them. When you smear a substance on to something it is difficult to completely remove it from the object. You may remove some of it. You even may remove most of it. But there will always be a residue or stain from the smearing. When God anoints you, He smears His ability upon you. You'll know when someone is anointed for a task or an assignment; you will see the stain of God's power and presence upon them. The anointing of God is His "stamp of approval" on you to do what you are doing. See, if God didn't approve you to do it, then He will not anoint you to do it! Many of us are doing things that God never anointed or placed His stamp of approval on us to do. God is only obligated to anoint what He appoints. What has God anointed you to do? He has anointed you to do what He has assigned you to do. If you have been negligent in carrying out His plan for your life, repent and get back on track. It's not too late.

CHAPTER TEN

Qualifications of an Armor Bearer, Part II

Exodus 18:21-22
[21] Moreover thou shalt provide out of all the people able men, such as fear God, men of truth, hating covetousness; and place such over them, to be rulers of thousands, and rulers of hundreds, rulers of fifties, and rulers of tens:
[22] And let them judge the people at all seasons: and it shall be, that every great matter they shall bring unto thee, but every small matter they shall judge: so shall it be easier for thyself, and they shall bear the burden with thee.

Moses led Israel out of Egypt and now they are in the wilderness heading to Canaan. Some theologians believe that this exodus of the nation of Israel numbered about 3 million people. Can you imagine pastoring 3 million people?! One can only imagine the number of problems they brought to Moses. The Bible says that Moses would hear people's problems from morning to evening. Moses' father-in-law, Jethro, asked him, "What are you doing? You are going to wear away." So Jethro gave Moses a plan. He said to set men as judges over groups of thousands, hundreds, fifties, and tens. They will handle the small matters but you will handle the great matters. These men were assigned to lift a load from Moses, ultimately destroying the attack of the enemy. These men possessed the spirit of an armor bearer. Jethro gave Moses the qualifications for selecting the men. Let's take a look at them.

VII.   Fear God

Jethro's first qualification was to select men who fear God; men who reverence and respect God. When one fears God he or she is honoring God. Honor is placing proper value on something or someone. These men honored God by making Him priority in every area of their lives. In other words, it doesn't matter where I am or who's with me, God is "numero uno." Men and women who fear God do not live one way at home and another way at church. They don't have a double standard. Pleasing God is more important than pleasing man.

In the book of Ecclesiastes, Solomon is nearing the end. He has lived an interesting life. He had riches beyond our imagination. He had the privilege of building God a house that was like none other. He is considered the wisest man who ever lived. He had 700 wives and 300 girlfriends! His name was known all over the world. He had seen a lot and experienced a lot. Now the end was near. After seeing and experiencing life, he summarizes the essence of living in chapter 12. Many ask the question, what is life all about or what is my purpose? Ladies and gentlemen, brothers and sisters ask no more. The wisest man who ever lived gives us the answer. And it's found in verse 13.

Ecclesiastes 12:13 (KJV)
13 Let us hear the conclusion of the whole matter: Fear God, and keep his commandments: for this is the whole duty of man.

Solomon writes that when it is all said and done, the only thing that matters is fearing God and obeying God. It is giving God proper value in your life. Are you bestowing the proper value on God in your life? Are you honoring Him in your relationships, finances, thought life, etc.? Is He truly the King of your life or is someone or something else sitting on the throne of your heart? The choice is up to you.

VIII.   Men of truth.

Truth in this context is defined as stable, trustworthy, established and firm. Jethro is saying to Moses, seek out men who are not novices. Look for men who've been through something and have survived. Seek men who have been in battle and have the scrapes and scars to prove it; men who did not faint in the day of adversity, but stood when trouble came. The Bible says if you faint in the day of adversity, there was nothing to you in the first place (Pro. 24:10, MSG)! Jethro was encouraging Moses to look for men who bowed down to God and stood up to the devil! This type of man can only be found in the Word.

Psalms 1:2-3 (KJV)
2 But his delight is in the law of the Lord; and in his law doth he meditate day and night.
3 And he shall be like a tree planted by the rivers of water, that bringeth forth his fruit in his season; his leaf also shall not wither; and whatsoever he doeth shall prosper.

I can hear Jethro coaching his son-in-law and saying, "Moses, don't select trees that are weak and frail and will break during a storm. But select trees, Moses, which are "firmly" rooted in the soil of the Word. So that when the winds blow and the storms come, they will stand. Though they bend, they will not break!" When the winds of trouble and adversity begin to blow, pastors and leaders need men and women of truth who will stand with them; who will provide support to the leader as well as the church or ministry.

Men and women of truth will not break, because they are established and firmly settled in God's Word.

IX.   Hate covetousness.

When you look up the definition for covetousness it means an unhealthy desire for a person's possessions (i.e. car, home, clothes, spouse). As armor bearers, we should not covet. God is able to bless you just like He blessed your neighbor. When we desire another man's possession we hinder God in giving to us what is rightfully ours!   In Exodus, Jethro was referring to covetousness in a different context. He admonished Moses to look for men who hate dishonorable ways in which money is obtained. Search for men who will not take a bribe. It also means men who will not change their decisions for money. Do   you   hate covetousness? Can you be bought? Money is not the only currency.   Some people will compromise over a compliment or compromise to fit in or to be liked. Friend, I encourage you to hate covetousness. Do not sell out to people or to the Satan. The price you pay is more than you and I could ever afford. Decide to sell out to Jesus and His purpose for your life. I guarantee you that it will be worth it!

(Acts 6:1-4)
And in those days, when the number of the disciples was multiplied, there arose a murmuring of the Grecians against the Hebrews, because their widows were neglected in the daily ministration.

Then the twelve called the multitude of the disciples unto them, and said, It is not reason that we should leave the word of God, and serve tables.

Wherefore, brethren, look ye out among you seven men of honest report, full of the Holy Ghost and wisdom, whom we may appoint over this business.

But we will give ourselves continually to prayer, and to the ministry of the word.

Here we see the need for a person who ends, consumes, or utterly destroys the attacks of the enemy by lifting, bearing up or carrying away a particular load or burden from the leader. The apostles stated that they should not neglect preaching the Word of God to handle the widows. Their primary responsibility was the preaching of the Word. To leave that and handle the widows would not be the best and highest use of them for the Kingdom. Handling the widows was a good thing, but not a God thing. God called them to preach the gospel. The daily administrative duties should be handled by another. So the apostles told the church to select seven men with certain characteristics. The list is below.

X.   Honest report.

When the apostles used the term, honest report, what they were saying was select men who have good and attested character. They were not novices, but had been tested and proven. They were experienced in serving in all types of situations and conditions. And they served with excellence. Their reputation was above reproach inside of the church and outside of the church. The term, "honest report", is derived from the same root word as the word, martyr. A martyr is a person who believes in an idea or principle so strongly that they not only will live their life according to it, but they will even die for it. Armor bearers are men and women who are willing to die for their convictions. I am not necessarily referring to a physical death, but dying to your flesh and

> "Armor bearers with an honest report realize that they have to die daily to their fleshly desires to fulfill their duties of serving."

selfish desires. In order to serve effectively you cannot live according to the desires and appetites of your flesh. Armor bearers with an honest report realize that they have to die daily to their fleshly desires to fulfill their duties of serving. This is done by relying on the power of the Holy Spirit.

XI.   Full of the Holy Ghost.

Paul says choose men who are full of the Holy Ghost. Choose men who are influenced and controlled by God's Spirit. Galatians 5:16 says "This I say then, walk in the Spirit, and ye shall not fulfill the lust of the flesh." Ephesians 5:18 picks it up and encourages us not to be drunk with wine, wherein is excess; but be filled with the Spirit. If you are full of something, then you cannot be filled with another substance. If I fill a glass with water or with dirt, then I cannot fill it with something else. As it is in the natural, so it is in the spiritual. If we are filled with the Holy Spirit then malice, jealousy, backbiting and so on can't get in. What are you filled with today? Is the Spirit of God filling every place in your life? In other words, are you allowing the Holy Spirit to control every area of your life or do you allow Him to control some areas and the other areas you control? He wants total control of your life.

Your level of effectiveness as an armor bearer is commensurate with the level of control you give to the Holy Spirit in your life. Listen, don't be drunk or influenced by the wine of this world. Don't let the world's perspective control your stability in God. If you are not watchful, careful and prayerful you can become inebriated with the cares and perceptions of this world. People who become intoxicated

> "If you are not watchful, careful and prayerful you can become inebriated with the cares and perceptions of this world."

are unstable, physically and mentally. Your perception is skewed because of alcohol. You cannot view things in their proper context. That's why they say don't drink and drive. When you become drunk with the world's issues, mores and perceptions, you do not view life in its proper context. The proper context is according to God not the world. That is why you must consistently be filled with the Holy Spirit; so that you can maintain the proper perspective on your assignment and your life.

XII.   Wisdom.

Finally, the apostles write, choose men with wisdom. James 1:5 says, "If any of you lack wisdom, let him ask of God, that giveth to all men liberally, and upbraideth not; and it shall be given him." Wisdom can be defined as applying the right knowledge to the right situation at the right time. You can know the right things but apply it at the wrong time. Wisdom is more than knowledge or "know how." It involves "know when" and "know what." You can say the right thing at the wrong time. Wisdom is speaking the right word at the right time in the right situation.

I am reminded of Naaman, the captain of the king's army (II Kings 5). Naaman had leprosy. His wife's servant told him about the prophet, Elisha, in Israel who could heal him. So Naaman goes to the prophet's house expecting an audience with him. Elisha does not come to the door, but sends instructions to Naaman on how to receive deliverance from the leprosy. The instructions are dip seven times in the Jordan River. Naaman is furious. First of all, Elisha did not greet him. Naaman was expecting Elisha to speak a word over him

"Wisdom can be defined as applying the right knowledge to the right situation at the right time."

or lay hands on him. Secondly, Naaman said there are better rivers to dip in than the Jordan. He even offers the names of a few. In his rage, he walks away probably with the intention of not obeying the prophet. Then his servants say something that is life changing for Naaman. They said if he had told you to do something difficult or heroic you would have done it, but he simply said dip seven times and be clean (II Kings 5:13). Naaman listened to his servants and he was healed. Imagine what would have become of Naaman had the servants not spoke to him in his time of need. They spoke the right words at the right time for the right situation and it saved the life of their leader. Your words, your actions could be life giving and life changing to your leader.

Proverbs 4:5-13 (KJV)
5 Get wisdom, get understanding: forget *it* not; neither decline from the words of my mouth.
6 Forsake her not, and she shall **preserve** thee: love her, and she shall **keep thee**.
7 Wisdom *is* the principal thing; *therefore* get wisdom: and with all thy getting get understanding.
8 Exalt her, and she shall promote thee: she shall **bring thee to honour**, when thou dost embrace her. (emphasis added)

I have listed 12 qualifications of an armor bearer. The number 12 in scripture is symbolic of government or ruling. There are 12 months in a year, 12 inches equal 1 foot, 12 tribes of Israel and Jesus selected 12 disciples. The book of Revelation mentions the 24 (12X2) elders. Allow these 12 characteristics to govern you as you endeavor to become an effective armor bearer.

A Title or a Towel

So many Christians are more interested in a position in the Kingdom than they are working in the Kingdom. Christ shows us that grabbing a towel, which symbolizes work, serving, being attentive, is more appropriate than grabbing a title. Let us strive to be effective and not significant. You see significant people may be well-known people but do not impact lives for the better. Effective people, like Jesus, positively impact people's lives. Servers concentrate on being effective, not significant. They are not interested in being known. They are not interested in the spotlight. They are interested in helping people becoming better. Servers shine the spotlight on others and on Jesus. So my friend will you choose significance or effectiveness? Which one will you grab, a title or a towel? It is my hope that you will choose the latter.

ABOUT THE AUTHOR

Bishop T. Cedric Brown is a native North Carolinian. At a young age, he accepted Jesus Christ as his Lord and Savior. He received his initial spiritual training at Pelt Chapel Pentecostal Holiness Church. He acknowledged his call to the preaching ministry in 1988 and in May 1998 received his first ministerial license in The Mt. Calvary Holy Church of America, Inc. One year later, he was ordained an Elder.

In 1986, Bishop Brown received his Bachelor of Science Degree in Industrial Engineering from North Carolina A & T State University. In May 2001, he received a Master of Arts degree in Counseling and Human Services from Regent University in Virginia Beach, Virginia. In May 2008, he earned a Doctor of Ministry degree from United Theological Seminary in Dayton, Ohio with a concentration in Leadership Development and Organization Dynamics.

Over the past twenty years he has been blessed to serve under the dynamic leadership of Bishop Alfred and Co-Pastor Susie Owens. Bishop Brown has faithfully served the congregation of Greater Mount Calvary Holy Church (GMCHC), a progressive, inner-city church with an adult membership of more than 7,000. In recognition of his loyalty and diligence to the work of the ministry, in 2000, he was appointed as the Associate Pastor. He is responsible for providing oversight to the 61+ church ministries and directors.

Bishop Brown is a gifted teacher who, along with his wife, Rev. Bobette Brown, teaches a mid-week bible study. He also serves as an instructor for Calvary Bible Institute, an accredited Bible school that provides Christian education and preparation for persons desiring to effectively function in the Body of Christ. Further, he serves as the Director of the Men's Ministry. In March 2008, he was honored to be appointed Dean of the Adjutant's Academy of the Joint College of African-American Pentecostal Bishops. Bishop Brown was consecrated a Bishop in the Lord's Church during the Annual Holy Convocation of the Mt. Calvary Holy Church of America, Inc. in August 2008. Two years later he was elevated to the office of Second Vice-Bishop of the organization. In 2012, Bishop Brown was honored to be appointed the Jurisdictional Bishop over the state of Florida.

He has been serving in full-time ministry since 1994. He began his career with GMCHC as the Administrative Assistant to the Senior Pastor. However, through his dedication and outstanding work performance, he was promoted to an executive managerial position. In this capacity, he oversees the directors for the external entities of GMCHC. His area of oversight includes: the GMC Bookstore; Calvary's Alternative to Alcohol and Drug Addiction Center; the Bishop Alfred A. Owens, Jr. Family Life Community Center; and, Calvary Bible Institute.

Bishop Brown's partner in marriage and ministry is his wife, Rev. Bobette D. Greene Brown. They are the proud parents of two sons – Joshua and Caleb.

For more information on the ministry of Bishop T. Cedric Brown, contact us at,

Greater Mt. Calvary Holy Church
610 Rhode Island Avenue, NE
Washington, DC 20002
202-529-4547
Bishoptcb@gmail.com

 Follow me **@bishoptcb**

 Follow me **@Bishop T. Cedric Brown**